EBook Millionaire

Your Complete Guide to Making Money Selling EBooks Online

Copyright Information

Copyright 2013 by Ebook Millionaire

Information in this product is the property of the author. No part of this book may be duplicated, resold, copied, stored in a retrieval system, transmitted in any form or by any other means, electronic, photocopy or otherwise or reproduced without prior written permission from the author. Unauthorised duplication of this material in any form is strictly prohibited. Violators will be prosecuted to the fullest extent of the law.

This book is for your personal enjoyment and education only. If you would like to share this book with another person, please purchase an additional copy for each recipient. If you are reading this book and did not purchase it, or it was not purchased exclusively for you please return and purchase your own copy. Please respect the hard work of the author.

If you have any information regarding the copying of this material, please report it to
james@ebookmoneymaker.com

Disclaimer

The author assumes no responsibility for the use or misuse, damage and/or financial loss sustained to persons or property as a result of reading this book.

The use of this information should be based on your own due diligence and you agree that our company is not liable for any success or failure you may have that is directly or indirectly to the purchase and use of our information.

***

Contents

Introduction
- Think you can't write a book?
- This is an incredible opportunity...
- Grab Your Killer Blueprint

Chapter 1 Why self publish?
- Finally power to the people!
- 4 trends to take advantage of:
- Success Stories
- Reasons a book does NOT sell:
- The best risk free business!
- Exponential Growth in your existing business
- Do I Have To Be A Great Author?
- Manage and control your empire

Chapter 2: 3 Essential Steps to Take BEFORE you start writing! (Most authors fail here.....)
1. Market Research
   - Capturing Ideas
   - Power of Clickbank
   - Adwords
2. Know Your Audience
3. Develop your strategic plan
   - Write an outstanding book

Chapter 3: Marketing that Sizzles!
- Essential Marketing Tools for Success
- Twitter
  - What is Twitter?
- Write a winning blog
  - What is a blog?
  - Do I really need a blog?
  - What do I include on my blog?
- The 5 secrets to get readers addicted to your blog:
- Getting serious traffic

Chapter 4: How To Master the Power of Facebook Marketing

   Step 1: Set yourself up for major success

   Step 2: Go viral

   Step 3 Give your page personality

   Step 4 Create a content calendar

   Step 5 Put on a show

     Track and Measure

Chapter 5 Critical Internal Marketing (most authors do not know this!)

   E Book Cover

   A clever title is worth a million dollars

   Formatting and Publishing

   The 3 Best Conversion Tools

   Creating a table of contents designed to sell

   Links

   What about pictures?

   Royalties and pricing

   Clever Pricing Strategy

   Perceived value of the product

   Create your author page on Amazon Author Central

   Enrol in the Amazon KDP select program

   Look Inside Feature

   Get amazing reviews- every time!

Chapter 6 Are other traditional forms of marketing any good?

   Forums

   Press releases

   Blog links

   More Social Media- do I need to do ALL of it?

Chapter 7 Neglected parts to most businesses

   Outsourcing

   Keep Expenses low

   Segment Your Day

CHAPTER 8: Here we go...!

   What can go wrong?

   What if it all goes right?

Introduction

Welcome to *E Book Millionaire*. This book is your fastest, quickest way to master the latest strategies for high level success selling your eBooks online, on Kindle or on any other self publishing platform. Whether you want to replace your full time income, supplement your existing income, help launch your public speaking career or sell your other products on the back of your book success, *e Book Millionaire* will help you. Now is the greatest moment in time to take advantage of this great opportunity open to all of us. The costs of self publishing are next to nothing, you no longer need to find an agent and you can do it all part time from the comfort of your home.

But simply publishing an e-book does not guarantee success. Many thousands of e-book authors never sell one copy and their books languish at the bottom for the sales rankings for years.

Do NOT let this happen to you!

For most authors, it is a lack of marketing knowledge rather than poor writing skills that result in poor sales. Assuming you can write a great book, it is also your job to sell it. This means getting your book in front of as many buyers as possible. *E Book Millionaire* will teach you the secrets of "internal marketing" within the Amazon Kindle system to ensure your book is found for relevant searches as well as the little known secrets of "external marketing" to attract thousands of non Kindle readers to your books. *E-Book Millionaire* will also help you if you just want to publish one or two books or whether you wish to start a full time publishing empire with multiple titles across many genres.

I will give you the simple formula you need to get your book flying up the best seller lists within 30 days and get your book found by the millions of people searching for your information or entertainment every day.

The size of this market is immense. According to Mashable.com in 2011 e-book sales were $3.2 billion in 2011; they are forecast to be $9.7 billion by 2016. Even if you can grab just a small fraction of this pie, you will be financially secure and have the time freedom you need to spend time doing what you really want to do! Jeff Bezos of Amazon stated in January 2013 that e-book sales have jumped 70% year on year from 2011-2012. This is not just pocket money guys, this is an massive opportunity-well within your reach. Did you know Amazon now sells MORE e-books than printed books?

The best thing about this business is that this income is passive! Once you have sales rolling in, they can keep coming in for years- month in, month out. On top of that you can increase your income at least five fold by using other strategies that I will show you in later chapters. Do the work once, get paid for it and keep getting paid week in, week out while you are asleep. This is a smart business to be in!

Think you can't write a book?
Everyone has different skills and talents and we love to learn from each other. If you enjoy something, the chances are there is a whole group of other people who will be equally passionate about your subject matter too and will be desperate to hand you over some money to be entertained or to

read your pearls of wisdom. Life in the digital and the e-book world moves at a frightening pace. You need to understand the latest strategies and tools for staying at the top of this game and that is what I will teach you.

Now is the time to get involved, write and publish the novel you have always dreamed of writing. Earn a second income from your existing skills and knowledge base by sharing it with the world. Fiction, non-fiction, how-to or short stories, whatever you want to write, in any niche, there will be an audience. My job is to show you how to successfully reach these people and make sure you start with a pool of "hungry" buyers who are desperate for the information in your book. As a $100 billion plus market cap e-commerce juggernaut, Amazon already has a substantial user base. 282 million people visited Amazon in 2011 (that equates to 20% total internet traffic). If you can get your book in front of these millions of eye balls, your future is pretty well set up! Listen up folks- Amazon already has the buyers! We don't need to look for buyers. They come every day to Amazon market place in their millions. The hard work has been done. We just need to show up and I will show you a few clever strategies to make sure your name and your book are in the right place!

When I started writing books, my process was a bit random to be honest. Well actually, the truth is I did not have a process! I just wrote about what I thought people might like to know, then crossed fingers and prayed someone would buy it. Guess what? I sold a few copies but hardly anything to boast about.

Eventually I changed my whole approach and started with the end in mind. I now consider my audience FIRST then write the book, knowing **before I start** that there are already thousands, if not millions of people seeking this precise information each and every month.

Guess what? My sales took off! And they remain consistent. I earn more in a month now than I did in a whole year. What's even better is that I can go on vacation for a month or two, knowing I am still earning great income without having to do anything!

And I will show you **my exact formula for success** in this book...

I will take you step by step on the journey that includes:

- What to do before you have even decided on your title
- Researching your market place (to be certain you have an excited pool of hungry buyers)
- Correctly formatting your book (simple but most beginners get this wrong)
- Sizzling external marketing (the step most authors fail miserably at)
- Clever internal marketing strategies (if you do not do these, you will fail)
- Extra ways to derive massive income from your books (BIG money is made here)

Like any new endeavour, there is a learning process. The learning process can be so time consuming, frustrating and miserable which is when most people give up. This book will condense this process for you in a way that you simply cannot fail. All you need to do is follow the steps and you will be way ahead of everyone else just starting out.

Self publishing is a business. You need to learn the **business** of writing and publishing.

In fact even if you have already published a couple of books that are not getting the sales you feel you deserve, then devour the marketing section of this book, follow the steps and you should be able to see your sales reach new heights you never thought possible.

I myself love writing, always have, always will. The e-book opportunities for me have changed my life. The old days of practically begging publishing houses for an interview so I could prostitute myself before them are long gone. I now control my own writing and publishing empire. I live and die by my sword (or rather my keyboard). The freedom is incredible.

Of course with great opportunity comes great responsibility. If I fail, I have no one else to blame but myself. It is now up to me to do all the jobs the publishing houses used to do: check the formatting, do the editing, devise a marketing plan, implement the plan, control sales, optimize search engines and of course make darn sure I write such a great book my readers tell all their friends to buy it.

However I am much more comfortable controlling my own destiny, instead of waiting to hear whether "Jane" from the editing department has got back to work from her flu bug to decide whether my book is good enough for her readers.

This is an incredible opportunity...

The sales of Kindles and other e-book readers have been exponential over the last few years and guess what people with e-readers do?

Yes- They buy books!

E-book readers have brought many people back to reading who had previously given it up.

Kindle owners purchase four times as many books as they did before they bought a Kindle. It's brilliant! No more going to the shops, finding they are out of stock, ordering your book and waiting a couple of weeks by which time your excitement, momentum and drive may have eroded. Waiting for two weeks now in our lifetime is forever! The convenience of e-books is fabulous- instant books at the click of a button!

Time moves so fast – we need information NOW and we want it NOW!

The growth in Kindle and e-book readers is set to explode over the next few years. So I advise you to jump on board, get set up for massive passive income as long as you read this book, take action and do it right.

Grab Your Killer Blueprint

Consider this a killer blueprint for writing, marketing and publishing successful e-books.

All I ask from you is that you take immediate ACTION. The problem for many people is they do not jump in straight away and get started. Sometimes the path ahead is not always clear so people do nothing and continue doing insane amounts of research and making the task ahead appear so big that they never get started.

Please promise me that you will take some notes along the way, generate ideas as you go along and jump right in. Even if you cannot yet see the path ahead fully illuminated. Even if you can see a glimmer of light and a possibility of success, go for it and commit fully. Assuming you write a great book, the income will continue to increase as more and more people switch to digital books.

So let's begin, I know that this book can change your financial life if you let it, so in good faith, I wish you every success and joy ahead and I am so excited for you and the journey you are about to take.

To your enormous success!

James

Chapter 1 Why self publish?

Finally power to the people!

For the first time in history YOU can write, edit, publish and market your own book direct to your readers from your bedroom at next to no cost.

Remember the agony writers went through in days gone by (not so long ago). They would spend a year or two toiling and slaving over their manuscript. Then spend months and months through the agonising editing process, crafting and refining their masterpiece only to have it then rejected by 80 publishing houses and tossed on the scrapheap. For some, the process was so painful that they never put pen to paper again. Others would go into a deep depression for a few months, before picking themselves up and starting over in the hope that their next work would find favour.

We however are blessed to live in different times. We have immense freedom to speak, write and earn a part time income, a full time income, or mega bucks through our writing. The choice is in your hands. Of course the writing must be great, the story compelling, the information top quality and it has to provide value to the reader. This goes without saying. You must not and cannot put "drivel" out there and expect to earn good money. You will be found out quickly and your reputation tarnished.

Instead if you focus on quality, your readers will come back for more, and you will develop a solid fan base who will buy anything that you have written.

These changes are very recent. Self publishing used to be a taboo subject. It was not talked about often as it was a last resort. People who self published were considered failed authors because they could not find an agent or get their book published by a publishing house. They would scrape together several thousand dollars to publish a print run themselves and try to sell their book alone. Not many succeeded and it was a very difficult and very expensive way to reach your target audience.

Luckily the world has changed and authors that already have successful hard back and paperback books are scrambling to get their books onto electronic format and push it out to the millions of loyal fans who have Kindles, Nooks, IPads and other e-readers. Even the traditional publishing houses are having to jump on board. Publishing giant Random House has revealed that 20% of sales last year were from digital books. E-books are without doubt becoming more and more popular. E-readers are cheaper, environmentally friendly, convenient and much lighter to take on holiday. The advantages to the author and to the consumer are massive. The cost to the consumer is less and the royalty checks to the author are more as the middle man has been cut out.

4 trends to take advantage of:

All we have to do is open our eyes to what is happening around us and join in. These trends are only going one way!

1. Book retail stores are disappearing from the high street. Many are going bankrupt as readers switch to electronic formats.
2. Big publishing houses are losing their power and their stranglehold on the industry.
3. Downward pressure on book prices as paper backs have to compete with e-books which have a low cost of delivery.
4. Authors communicate directly with their readers via social media developing huge loyal fan bases and control over the relationship.

Success Stories

Several self-published authors have sold over 1 million e-books in less than 1 year and many of these were unknown authors who would never have had a publishing deal from a traditional publisher. Think about the royalty check for that!

One of the most well-known cases is Amanda Hocking, a 20-something from Minnesota, who writes young adult fiction in the vampire, paranormal romance genres. She has made over $2 million dollars from e-books in just over a year. No publisher would touch her originally but now she has a bidding war with the 4 big publishing houses offering her another $2 million to sign with them for the next 4 books! She has also sold movie rights to one of her novels.

Or John Locke who was the first self published author to sell 1 million e-books- and he did it in just 5 months!

Or J.A. Konrath who started in 2009 by putting his "out of print books" for sale as e-Book's. He writes in the mystery and thriller genre. By 2010 he was selling 100 books a day and earning $43,000 a year "sitting on his butt". He now earns five-six figures **a month.**

Or Stephen Leather, a British journalist who by 1992 was already was a successful novelist. He self published the books that traditional publishers did not want, priced them at 99 cents and promoted them by posting on forums. Within 3 months he had knocked Stieg Larsson off the top spot and is now #2 best selling Kindle fiction author behind Lee Childs.

These are awesome success stories and proves that you do not need to be a known author, just a bit of clever marketing and a darn good read can get you there.

Reasons a book does NOT sell:

There are clear reasons why a book does not sell. When I do my consulting work to help authors increase their sales and dominate their niche these are the most common reasons that have not been addressed.

They seem obvious now- but at the time the author simply has no idea why their incredible book is not selling. Notice only one of them has to do with the actual writing!

- It may just not be very good
- It may be poorly formatted
- It may have a dull, uninspiring cover
- It may have a boring title
- It may be full of spelling errors and poor grammar
- The author may have done no marketing and it never actually gets seen by potential readers

Throughout this book I will teach you what to do to excel in each of these areas.

The best risk free business!

Most business incurs a cost of start-up. Think about it- maybe you require $100,000 minimum to buy a business, or buy the franchise, kit the business out with stock or infrastructure, pay for a shop fit, employ staff, pay rent, rates, power, develop your brand, market your product or service and that is all before you have made one sale!

This is very tough, a massive gamble and a very big financial risk.

Most businesses open their doors "hoping" to get customers, and "hoping" the customers like their "stuff". And what's worse is that the consumer is fickle, so even if they liked your stuff last year, they might not want it this year.

Another top reason to write books is there are no employees!

Anyone who has had employees knows this is music to their ears. No employee tribunals, no holiday pay, no sick pay, no insurance and no maternity or paternity pay. Simply heaven!

E-books electronic format also means no unsold stock. I do know people who could not find a publishing house in the old days but they believed in their book so much that they spent $20,000 of their hard earned cash to do a print run and do some marketing themselves. They printed 5000 copies, and unfortunately 15 years later, they have sold only 87 books and the rest are cluttering up their garage collecting dust.

In the e-book world the cost of entry is minimal and the risk is minimal. As you will see I will show you exactly what to do to ensure that BEFORE you start that you know you WILL have readers looking for your book. How great is that?

There is a way to practically guarantee you will have a huge pool of buyers desperate to hand over their money to get your information. I will show you this in a later chapter.

Cost of entry to most traditional businesses is approximately $100,000.

Cost of entry to e-book self publishing is approximately $200!

Which would you rather?

Exponential Growth in your existing business

Of course many of you may not want a full time profession as an author. One of the big reasons many people write a book is to prove authority in their chosen profession. For example you may be a speaker or an engineer or an architect. Many people are seen as an expert in their field if they are introduced as author of "Architecture for New England Style Homes" or "Engineering Secrets of the Panama Canal".

From simply having written and published a book, they find they generate more architect appointments, or get more engineering jobs or invitations to speak. It is another great marketing tool and good source of leads.

The other way people use their book to enhance their existing business is to write a book at minimum cost to the consumer i.e. free or 99 cents. The purpose of the book is to provide such valuable or compelling information or such a great story that customers are driven to your website to find out more about you or find out more about your products, services or other books.

Once they are on your website you must aim to capture their email address then you can communicate with them at regular intervals and tempt them with higher priced products or services as now, you know they like you and what you have to say.

This is a very low cost way of gaining new customers or warm leads. Customers will ONLY bother to visit your website if they like your initial book but if they do, you know the person already wants to engage with you.

The opportunities to create a new business or expand your existing business are limitless.

Do I Have To Be A Great Author?

As consumers, we are now extremely media savvy and very demanding of our entertainment- we can afford to be choosy.

You must remember that so much information is out there for free. Why would someone pay to read your book? They will if they believe you have specialist knowledge to help them solve a problem quickly, or are able to entertain them with a gripping tale.

As the cost of entry is minimal- the cost to consumer is minimal. As you will see as we go through the process, most books are priced between £2.99-£9.99. Many sell for £0.99. This means instead of the reader having to think "Is this latest book worth £10?", all they have to think now is "that sounds vaguely interesting and what the heck it is only $2.99! I will give it a go!"

In other words you do not have to have the language skills of Shakespeare. BUT you do have to be effective and entertaining. You do not have to be able to conjugate every verb in the subjunctive tense but you do have to be able to chat to people and engage them in conversation through a gripping tale with intriguing characters if your book is fiction or effective solid information if your book is nonfiction.

Manage and control your empire

This book will teach you everything you need to know whether you just want to publish one book or whether you wish to make it your career to build, grow and manage a publishing empire. You can market other people's books for commission, develop a few of your own bestselling titles or a combination of the two.

Just a quick note to manage expectations: will you make a million dollars in your first week? Of course not! But every empire starts with one sale. Most successful authors see a gradual increase in sales as different elements kick in like word of mouth marketing, or getting more and more reviews and testimonials, your website getting more traffic, your Twitter account engaging with more and more fans. The marketing will be covered in detail in a later chapter but focus on starting and following the process. Do it right and with millions of buyers out there, the sales potential is almost unlimited.

So I hope you are convinced by now that this opportunity is simply too good to resist.

Let's get started with the detail, the nitty gritty, the system that will help you have amazing success...

Chapter 2: 3 Essential Steps to Take BEFORE you start writing! (Most authors fail here.....)

1. Market Research

The old adage goes "everyone has a book inside them". Whist this may be true, if your goal is to sell thousands of books, it makes sense to make sure there are thousands of people who already want your book.

Market research is paramount to success. For most authors if you write a random book, it is not likely to do very well. How much better is your success likely to be if you KNOW you have a pool of hungry buyers desperate to get their hands on your book or your information?

Start looking at what buyers are *already* buying or what they are *already* looking for.

This process is slightly different if you are writing fiction or nonfiction.

For **fiction** books, it is a great idea to be "on trend". Spend some time in the best seller lists and see if there are certain themes or genres that suit your style or that you particularly identify with. For example many books in the best seller lists now have a similar theme to "Fifty Shades of Grey" the best selling trilogy by E L James. Even though this series was very popular one year ago, books with a similar theme are still selling in their thousands. Prior to that books based on vampire themes were selling in their thousands. If you can piggy back on their success with a similar theme, you know thousands of readers are loving (and buying) these books right now.

Do not worry if your niche differs from these. You may specialise in detective stories, romance or thriller novels and this is fine. There is an audience for everyone and sometimes niche subjects gather a huge, almost "cult" following and sell very well.

The point is to know your theme, your genre and your audience. If you do not have a burning desire to be in a certain niche- it may be a sensible idea to put yourself in a niche that millions of readers are already screaming out for.

Ask yourself these questions:

- Who is my audience?
- What do they want?
- What emotions do they wish to feel?
- What characters do they like?
- What is their driver to purchase my book?
- What will they get out of my book?

There are always trends, fads, fashions in all genres and it will make your life a whole lot more rewarding if your book flies off the shelves (or more accurately off the download list) and straight into the best seller lists!

For **nonfiction books** start to think about your skills, your hobbies, what interests you, what are you already an expert in? What are your passions?

Also spend time looking at the best selling lists and see if you identify with anything. Think about common problems people have and possible solutions to those problems. Read and absorb as much as you can. Spend time looking at the reviews of the best sellers and the book descriptions. You want to get a feel for the market, what sells and what doesn't.

How many nonfiction books end up in the top 10?

What is the average price of a bestselling Kindle book?

What do the best selling Kindle book covers have in common?

How many reviews do the best sellers have?

Read all the 4-5 star reviews and find out what they have in common.

What is it that most people like enough to comment on?

Then go to the bottom of the 1-2 star reviews: What are the factors that make people complain?

What are these books missing?

How exactly are they disappointing the reader?

You are seeking to give people what they want right now. Your market research will tell you what is selling and what is not.

Another way to get confirmation of what buyers are searching for is to use Google keyword tool.

www.**googlekeywordtool**.com/

This is a brilliant free tool that allows you to see how many people search per month for a particular term.

Compile a list of keywords that you think customers may be searching for. It may be 1 word to a 4 words phrase.

For example: if you are interested in car maintenance; you might type in "car maintenance", "fixing cars", "home mechanics", "DIY mechanic", "how to fix my car" and see what turns up.

Quite often the results are surprising. You can clearly see how many people are searching for this phrase on a monthly basis.

If you can provide a solution to their problem and there are already 950,000 people are month looking for solutions, you know you are onto a winner! A good rule of thumb is over 10,000 searches a month.

This is an incredible tool and a very useful exercise. If you are thinking of writing a book in a niche that no one is searching for, it is a good time to re think and come up with a niche that many thousands of people are searching for each month. You will save yourself months of agony in writing and marketing a book that maybe no one wants right now.

If it is your first book, it is even more important to ensure it is a success. This will give you confidence to continue and faith that you CAN do this. If you know before you even start chapter one that you will have thousands of potential buyers for your book, it just makes the whole process worthwhile.

Google keyword tool also throws up similar key phrases that you may not have thought of. This is also extremely useful and will give you awesome ideas for chapter headings. If you think you know a subject so well you could write few books in the niche, this will give you an idea for other book titles as well. If you come across a great niche, make a note of the top phrases people are searching for and keep them handy to use as chapter headings and key words in your marketing.

This is called search engine optimisation where you aim to include specific key words throughout your text and chapter headings that you know people are typing into the search engine box. As well as cleverly giving the buyer exactly what they want, it will help greatly with your marketing efforts as when they type in their search terms to Google, your book is more likely to pop straight up as you exactly match their criteria.

The other brilliant service is that Google keyword tool also shows you how competitive the phrase is and whether lots of other authors and marketers are competing for this phrase. The ideal scenario is lots of searches with low competition.

Remember even though you are keen to get writing and get your book published, market research is crucial and you need to spend time researching your market and developing your key words and key phrase list. If you are in such a rush to get your book out there, that you skip this stage, you could be doing a whole lot of work for nothing.

Here is an example below:

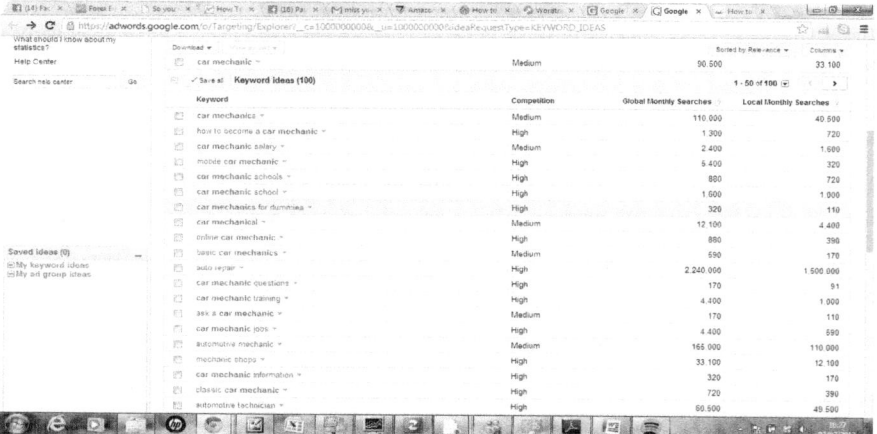

This example shows: the term "car mechanic" has 90,500 global monthly searches. This is pretty good. But notice if you changed the word in your title or chapter heading to "automotive mechanic" there are 165,000 global monthly searches. That change of word by itself might yield to a doubling of your sales.

You can also scour through the list quickly to find other chapter heading ideas.

In this example you can see the term "mobile car mechanic" only has 5,400 monthly searches but "automotive technician" has 60,500 searches. This process does not take long but you can see the value in giving you confidence that you are on a winner early on. It also gives you ideas that you may not have thought of that people are very interested in, which can help focus your mind and give you some clarity.

You need to know before you even put pen to paper that this book will sell. As I said earlier, there are thousands of books on Amazon Kindle that have not sold one copy! There are also thousand of books on Amazon that have only sold two copies and that is to their mother and their best friend!

So make the best use of your time and ensure you have a hungry pool of eager buyers out there before you sit down to write your masterpiece.

Make sure you know it will be profitable BEFORE you start!

Capturing Ideas

Get into the habit of looking for ideas everywhere. Ideas come to you all the time-in the shower, walking the dog, standing in a queue for the shopping, it is just a question of whether you notice them or not. You will generate more ideas being out and about than sitting in front of a white screen scratching your head.

Keep a notebook handy to write ideas down when they come to you at random times. Or use the voice recorder on your phone to keep hold of ideas. Your subconscious brain is trying to solve your problems all the time, make sure you listen to it!

If you have already built up a loyal Facebook, Twitter or blog following, you can ask your readers for ideas on what they would like to hear next from you. Or you can test book titles on them. Many authors write a mini- article on one of the potential subjects for their next book and see how many time it is liked on Facebook or shared with friends. The most popular article is the winner and will be the subject of their next book. This is very powerful and you need over 100,000 followers or fans for this to be very helpful. I will go into detail in a later chapter about how to leverage social media strategies.

Friends are often a good source of information too. Listen to your friends, what they talk about, what they get excited about, problems that they cannot find an answer to then do your research and see if these same subject areas are problems for a lot of people.

It could be your next bestseller!

Power of Clickbank

Click bank is a massive marketplace for digital products. This is relevant for nonfiction writers. Whilst you may or may not wish to list your book here, it is a significant source of information and research into what is selling and what buyers want. It is also another valuable source of potential ideas for you. Remember to sell your book, you must go where the buyers are. There are millions of people going to Click bank to look for digital information products.

http://www.clickbank.com

Spend 30 minutes browsing on what is selling, related products in your niche and how much competition you have. This is valuable time spent confirming your initial thoughts and narrowing down your niche.

It may give you fantastic ideas of a similar topic that you can piggyback off and share someone's existing customer database. For example if someone may have a successful book titled "Classic Cars", you may be thinking of doing a series of books on "Classic Jaguars", "Classic Rolls Royce's" and Classic Bentleys", you could contact them and request to share their email list for a share of profits.

Or if the top 3 books selling at the moment are on the similar theme "How to set up your successful catering business" you know a large percentage of people are interested in this and can write a similar book in this genre. You already know people are buying it. Your job is NOT to copy them but come up with a new angle, to make your book more enticing, more attractive and more informative.

Do not be afraid if other people already have books on this topic- so you think there will be no room for your book. There is ALWAYS room for the next good book.

Think of all the diet books out there... people still keep buying them looking for the latest "secrets" to weight loss! Come up with a unique angle and think how you can deliver the most value to your reader.

Contrary to popular thought- if there are NO books selling in your particular genre, beware as it may be because others have tried and failed. It is best and easiest to go where there is already a proven market place. Remember you want the reader to LOVE your book and be desperate to buy your next one. You want them to join your blog, your Facebook page, become a Twitter follower. It is so much easier and cheaper to market to an existing fan/customer than to find new ones all the time. Someone who already likes you and had a great experience is 80% more likely to buy from you again over someone who does not know you yet.

Adwords

If you are really in the testing mood, Google ad words allows you to test very cheaply whether people really want to pay for this information. It allows you to get compare book titles and see which ones are clicked on most. This is relevant for nonfiction writers.

You can set up an Ad word campaign, with the headline of your book or subject area for example "classic Cars" and direct customers to a holding page or an email capture page to grab their emails. Some authors may have a short story for download or a product related to their book for sale, or a free YouTube video on there with information. It is easy to set up and take down when you have seen the results in a few days to a week.

Check it out here:

https://adwords.google.com

Google has taken the time to provide excellent training on their website.

This distinguishes clearly whether people are just browsing for free information or whether they actually want to pay for high quality information.

2. Know Your Audience

Think about your audience- who they are, what they want and then give it to them!

This is especially relevant for fiction authors.

Nonfiction authors will be more reliant on keyword tools covered above, to know that they have a pool of hungry buyers. For fiction authors you need to define your audience and work out how you will reach them. Remember, without an audience, your book is worthless.

Be able to answer these questions quickly and clearly:

Who is your audience?

What age, sex and demographic are they?

What messages do they want?

What can I offer them?

What characters do they relate to?

Violence or romance? Fast paced or gentle?

Take the time to answer these questions in detail. Create a detailed outline of the whole book. Map out everything from the introduction to the conclusion. Also outline the tone, the style and the content of each chapter. Plan the character back stories- know them so well you know what makes them tick and you know what they will do in every situation. As you are writing you may think "would this character really say that or do that? Would they act that way?"

Outline plot lines and plausible scenarios before you write a single word of the book. As you read novels you like, observe and make notes on how good writers create tension, withhold information to create suspense and write gripping dialogues.

This process may take a few weeks but is worth every minute. You need to be congruent throughout the book.

3. Develop your strategic plan

As with anything you wish to be successful with in life, develop a plan. Just sitting down and staring at a random blank white screen and wondering how you can possibly string together 40,000-100,000 words that will entice an audience is pretty daunting!

Instead break down the task into manageable chunks. Schedule how many days you will write per week, how many words per day, a date by when you will finish each chapter and when you will finish the book. Focus on it until it is done. Sometimes authors do take many years to finish one book. Do not allow this to happen to you. Set a finish date in mind and exclude all other distractions until this is done. Create a writing schedule then stick to it. This is the discipline required to be a good writer. Many people think of a good idea, but then give up half way. Do NOT do that. Push through the difficult times and just keep going!

Remember in old fashioned publishing world, publishers would not even look at you if you did not have three or four books ready to roll out. Do the same for yourself. Keep writing! Even if the first book is not a major hit, keep going. You may need to come back and review the chapters in this book. You may have left something out in a rush. You may need to get more followers on Twitter or engage with your Facebook fan page more or update your blog. Make sure you are doing the basic things right. One strategy may be to develop a theme and become the expert in your niche with two or three books on the same subject matter.

If you are writing fiction and you will have taken the time to develop a strong character that readers love- keep writing other books using this character. This helped to create a massive fortune for E.L. James and her "Fifty Shades of Grey" series. Readers who loved the first novel and the lead character, Christian Grey did not hesitate to buy the next 2 books. They could not get enough.

The same theme works for nonfiction books too. If you have success in a certain niche, you can quickly write another 2-3 books in this area. It is likely that your readers will become loyal fans and want to know more about related areas. For example if I write a book on "Developing Magnetic Self Confidence" my readers who enjoyed this book might also buy the next book by me titled "Hypnosis for Self Confidence" or "Self confidence and Public Speaking". I have positioned myself as the expert in this field. (Hint: they might also buy a CD for self confidence or a DVD related to this topic)

Readers do prefer authors with multiple titles.

Remember though, to complete this process carefully, properly and with thought and care. If you write your first book well then quickly publish the next 2 books without editing, checking and proof-reading, you will be found out, get terrible reviews and have failed. The bad reviews for your subsequent books will also detract from your sales of your first great book.

Content is king, always produce quality!

Write an outstanding book

Once the research is over, you have decided on your niche, your topic, your genre, your characters, you need to get busy with the writing.

Make sure your book has a beginning, middle and end. For fiction novels your goal is to have your readers engage with the characters, to have such a gripping tale that they are disappointed when it ends, to have such passion and emotion oozing from each page that it is intoxicating right up until the last sentence.

For nonfiction books the structure is very important. Present the information in a logical but compelling way. Make the effort to provide a table of contents to help readers understand what your book offers them and help them quickly find the information they need. Then brainstorm every chapter with the major points you wish to write.

Sometimes you may find one or more chapters could be another book in itself. Make a note of this as this could be book number two. It is better to market a string of books ready to roll out and get well known as the expert in the subject matter as I mentioned earlier.

This is not a chapter on HOW to write a book. This topic is a whole book in itself and will differ enormously from genre to genre and from fiction to nonfiction. So for those of you who do need some guidance in this area, there are plenty of brilliant and helpful books on this topic. Some writers also get great benefit in joining a writers group; meeting like minded people and having the tutor correct or improve their work.

Chapter 3: Marketing that Sizzles!

Sadly many authors do not have a clue about marketing and sales.

This however is your massive advantage. Marketing is KEY to massive success. No one can buy your book if they are not aware of it! I am sure you have read books in the past that were very average but they had massive commercial success. I am sure you can also think of other books you have read that were simply brilliant but most people you know have never heard of them. The point is massive success does not come to the most brilliant writers but to the most brilliant marketers!

The next few chapters will be devoted to ensuring you know *exactly* what to do to get your book in front of as many potential buyers as possible. If you employ a few of these skills you will be ahead of most authors and have a very good chance of respectable and growing sales over a lifetime.

The first thing to do is have a marketing plan.

Set some goals. Define exactly what you actually want to achieve?

Be realistic and specific. Just to say "I want to be a millionaire" is admirable but the reality is if you do not set a specific, measurable goal, your brain will have nothing concrete to focus on and head towards. So an example might be something like: I will sell 3 books a week in January, 20 books a week in February, 60 books a week in March and get to 500 book sales a month by the end of the year.

Even if you *only* manage to sell 300 books at $2.99 this is still $897 a month. That is a pretty tidy sum for one little e-book! In many cases, it will be a LOT more than this.

Imagine if you have 10 books out doing these sales figures month in, month out whether you get out of bed or not. $8,970 a month passive income. What a great goal! And best of all it IS achievable and realistic! That is over $100,000 per year

It is worthwhile having multiple books out there. You will increase your chances of finding the winner by following the market research chapter above and spending time finding out what is "hot" in the market and what is already selling. Clever marketers do this all the time. They follow trends, the mood of the nation and produce products that people want. Rather than designing products THEN spending a fortune convincing people they want it.

Make life easy on yourself.

Essential Marketing Tools for Success

There are two main forms of marketing in the e-book world that we need to master: **External and Internal marketing.**

External marketing is marketing to the outside world through blogging, Twitter, Facebook, public speaking, radio interviews, press releases and anything else you can think of to get people to become aware of your book and buy it.

Internal marketing is the marketing you do *within* the Amazon market place to make sure that your book appears in the top 10 of whatever the search criteria the buyer has entered. Also internal marketing is crucial at this point to make sure that when the prospect has glanced at your book, you have done everything in your power to ensure that the buyer will stop long enough to read your cover, your book description and purchase it. It will also ensure that your book pops up as a suggested book to buy when the reader is browsing through your competitor's books.

This chapter covers external marketing, the next chapter covers internal marketing.

Twitter

Twitter is a social media platform which generates a high source of leads and sales for authors and must NOT be ignored. There are over 500 million active users on Twitter. You do need a Twitter account and know how to use it to draw a fraction of this population to your blog in order to buy your book.

Many successful businesses draw over $10, 000 a month revenue (and much more) purely from Twitter so it is worth spending some time getting this right.

What is Twitter?

Twitter is a free micro blogging service that connects you with the latest news, stories and information. Each tweet must be 140 characters or less. Twitter connects people with other like minded individuals, celebrities with their fans and businesses with their customers or partners. You can share photos, videos, latest blog posts, get feedback, interact and make new friends and fans. Businesses use it for branding, for sales and to deal with customer questions or complaints. If you still think it is just for John Doe to tell the world he had toast for breakfast, you are very far behind the curve!

Big business has realised the power of Twitter and is spending thousands of dollars engaging with their followers. If Twitter was simply an insignificant annoyance for teenagers with nothing better to do, they would not be throwing money at this.

Businesses like Dell, British Airways and Rolex have many thousands of followers and take the customer comments on Twitter very seriously. There are many incidents where a customer has complained about a business service on Twitter. Suddenly they are astonished to find they are immediately being called or tweeted from the President of the company asking how they could resolve their complaint. Twitter is so important that businesses have full time staff employed to constantly monitor every time their business name is mentioned on Twitter, responding immediately and constantly updating their Twitter accounts with the latest company news. Even the government and the Royal family are tweeting now!

Celebrities like Justin Bieber, Britney Spears, Stephen Fry and sports celebrities have millions of Twitter followers and generate millions of dollars in sales from these Twitter followers. They engage with their fans who feel like they get to know their favourite super star and engage with them directly. They are alerted where the star is at any one time, they sell records, books and gain huge followings.

So if it is good enough for them, it is good enough for us!

Here is the site:

https://twitter.com/

Like anything worthwhile, it does take time but is really worth it. If you have not set up a Twitter account, stop reading this, go and set one up. It is free and takes 5 minutes. In less than a week you should have a few hundred followers. You do a search for friends, celebrities you like, hash tags within your genre, keywords and click "follow" on all these people. Most of them will check you out and follow you back. It is a great way to engage with people and develop relationships. It works just like relationships in the real world. You cannot simply turn up to a party of people you have never met and expect them to like you instantly and buy your book. If you do this, people will block you from their life very quickly. Instead do not focus on your sales, focus on helping other people, asking questions, responding sincerely to other people. This will be appreciated and you will develop meaningful relationships. Later when you are ready to launch your book, your Twitter friends may be happy to give you a review or testimonial.

A quick word on hash tags: a hash tag is the # symbol. It is a quick way to group tweets together and make your tweet searchable. For example just after the crisis in Haiti, there were thousands of tweets on Haiti. If you wanted to see who was talking about it, you type in #Haiti to the search box and anyone who had used #Haiti would pop up on your time line.

Whenever you are writing your tweets, it is a good idea to start adding #hash tags wherever you can to make your tweet pop up as often as possible. Do a couple of searches yourself now to try it out.

If you have existing books out there, invite your fans to engage with you on Twitter. This is another valuable way of gaining feedback from your readers and suggestions about what they would like to hear about next.

Twitter used correctly is a massively valuable tool for drawing people to your website and gaining direct sales. As I mentioned before do not directly tweet "Come and buy my book" instead you might be more subtle like " Really excited today, I climbed from 238 to top 50 in sales ranking for my new book!" with a link to your website for those who wish to check it out. Also be helpful to these new friends and readers: go to their website, review their work, buy their book if it interests you and leave comments on their websites. People appreciate this activity and will be loyal to you for life.

On the left side of your Twitter home page there is a box called "trends". This changes all the time and shows you the top stories that people are tweeting about that day. See if you can think of a relevant link to the story of the day and one of your books or blog post. This is a really clever way of catching the attention of a whole new audience, especially the media.

By following other people who are in your niche or genre you can easily add more and more people into your sphere. You can search for more people with specific hash tags or interests. Providing you supply interesting or helpful content, they will re-tweet your messages then others will follow you and so your community grows. This is not a quick win- but important to get started on early. Imagine in 3 years time when you have a loyal fan base of 85,000 people and you announce the launch of your latest novel and instantly 5,000 people (or more!) go straight away to your site or to Amazon and download your latest book.... very powerful!

Best of all it is free- massive power to you!

Use it!

Write a winning blog

What is a blog?
A blog is a form of website that is arranged in reverse chronological order so the most recent post (piece of news) is seen first. It is short for weblog. It is usually updated regularly and contains recent, up to date information on a particular topic, and an archive of older articles and posts. Because it is updated so frequently it usually ranks very highly on the search engines as the content is continually changing. Also your aim will be to get some interaction from your fans and followers. So a blog becomes not simply a monologue, but a conversation.

A website however is usually static, containing information about the company, how to contact them, where their offices are, key benefits- it is a sales document or brochure, a blog is an interactive developing beast!

Do I really need a blog?
The simple answer is YES!

Your blog is the central hub of your marketing wheel. Every other tool feeds back to that. Your blog is very important. You need a blog to communicate with your readers and also to showcase your other offerings. It is the central hub of your empire. Of course you will still have the Amazon platform, your Twitter account and your Facebook page but central to all that is your blog. This is easy to set up. In the 21st century there is NO excuse not to have a blog. You need to buy a domain name, hosting and install wordpress www.wordpress.com

Take care over your domain name. Remember the keyword research you did at the beginning. You must include keywords where possible. The most important element of your blog being found is the domain name. Do not try to be too clever and obscure. Be straightforward and direct. Think about what the majority of your readers might be searching for and have those words in your domain name.

You can purchase your domain name and hosting from somewhere like www.godaddy.com or www.1and1.co.uk. The www.wordpress.com site will take you through in detail how to install a wordpress site onto your domain. If you are not technically minded, simply find a nephew, niece or a university student to help. Alternatively hire someone from www.guru.com or www.elance.com to set all this up for you. It will take them about 10 minutes to do and will not cost you much at all.

The most important thing is to get this step done quickly- Do not let this step take 3-4 weeks of your life. Your job is to write fantastic books and market them to the buying public, not get bogged down in minute details of setting up a blog. The longer you are not taking action, the more money you are losing!

In this world of social media, readers love to interact with their author. They love to provide feedback, make comments, find out more about you and what makes you tick. You will generate a far greater level of loyalty if you have a blog than if you do not bother.

What do I include on my blog?

1) Email capture box

A very important element of your blog is an email capture box to capture your customer's email. Of course these days people are wary of giving out their email address for fear of being spammed and their email box being stuffed with dubious offers. So you should address these fears right away. You must let your buyers know that their details will be kept safe, they will never be spammed, their email address will never be sold to an external agency and that they can unsubscribe easily at any time.

You must also give them a reason to give you their email address. Offer them something (a free book, a free short story, a free excerpt from your latest book, the top 10 free tips about subject x) so they will give you their email address. You can then stay in touch. Of course you will not spam them but give them relevant information and occasionally let them know when you have a new book coming out that might interest them.

Again the email capture box is an easy step of copy and pasting some text onto your blog. Or if you are struggling, get someone to do it for you-it will take them less than 2 minutes.

My friends: the money is in the list. You MUST be creating a list of people who like you and love your books.

2) "Contact me" page

Make sure you have a "Contact Me" page on your blog so readers can leave thank you notes, fan mail, suggestions about character development, plot lines, the next books they would love to read from you. You will be surprised how helpful loyal fans can be. Your aim here is to convert loyal readers into loyal friends. Then over time turn these friends into buyers, then buyers into reviewers. If they email you saying they loved your book, reply asking if you can use their comments on your blog and book.

Your goal is to develop a large email list of loyal fans who will buy anything you write. Direct as many Twitter followers as you can to your blog to try to capture their email. Remember that only 10% of USA population owns an e-book reader. So selling your book via your own blog will allow you to reach the other 90% of the market who may love to read your book but do not have an e-book reader.

3) Add sizzling information they are dying to return to

You can add information about the characters, more information about your life, your interests, sporting goals, musical tastes- let your creativity run wild. But always remember to keep in mind who your audience is and what they might like to hear about or comment on.

Make sure you interact with similar blogs and try to link with as many people as possible. Search for other blogs in your niche through relevant keywords, Subscribe to other people's blogs. Add helpful or complimentary comments. Ask other authors for interviews, interact with them, link to their posts on your site and be part of a growing community. Read the blog of novelist J. A. Konrath (http://jakonrath.blogspot.co.uk/) who has been self publishing since 2004 and recording his experiences on the blog. Anyone considering self publishing should be reading Joe to understand the pros and cons of the self publishing world.

As well as being a genuine member of a group, you want as much brand recognition as possible, you want to be everywhere at once, get noticed and draw as many readers to your site to download your books directly and subscribe to your page so you can capture their email address and stay in touch.

Remember also that anything that is published on the internet is there forever! So even if you did an interview with an industry leader posted it to your blog and got no sales from it in week one, it will be there on the internet forever gradually making you four sales a day for the next twenty years and beyond.

Once you get noticed by this activity, others will ask to interview you-maybe even journalists. Be prepared for these opportunities. Try to prepare one or two themes you wish to get across and one or two sound bites that journalists love that will definitely get published and get you even more recognition.

Commercially a blog makes sense. When you have a new book or a new product, you will already have a list of raving fans. All you need to do is send one email and voila you will already have sales. It's genius!

Imagine having an email list of 1000 people who will buy anything you write? Awesome! What if you built that to 10,000 people or 100,000 people?

The 5 secrets to get readers addicted to your blog:

1) Ooze Personality

People love people. Make sure your blog seems like it was written by YOU. That you discuss your opinions, thoughts, ideas, little stories that made you laugh. Also remember a blog is a conversation so ask them questions, ask for feedback, ask if anyone else has been in this situation, had this experience or tried this recipe.

If you receive replies, please make sure you follow up and respond. There is nothing worse for a reader if they take the time to respond to you and then hear nothing back. They need to know their comment has been heard and appreciated. Also seeing a conversation appear helps encourage other readers to leave their comments.

An active site generates momentum and will ensure you will crush the competition.

2) Make your blog something they want to share

Your job is to make sure people rush back to your blog time and time again. Make sure you entice them, engage with them. Remember there is a lot of competition out there for every subject trying to catch the buyer's attention. For example if you thought of writing a running book or a recipe book, there are so many other books and blogs on the subject that yours needs to be different, have a different angle and a reason why readers will listen to you above the din of other "experts" shouting at them. With a little thought, make sure you have an angle, create your own niche. Even though there is competition, it is NOT that difficult to be heard and stand out from the crowd. There IS room for your book but you do need to think about a unique angle. A fantastic and engaging blog will help distinguish your book – even more so if you share incredible information and demonstrate personality.

Create an "About Me" page with your photo and interesting facts about who you are and what makes you tick. You must post a blog or a short article several times a week that keeps your readers engaged and interested and shows them you are a passionate person interested in the same things they are. Take some time over your blog posts. You want to engage the reader and make them think "wow- this article/post is really cool. I will definitely check out his/her book".

Also add a subscribe button so readers get notified when you have uploaded a new post. Then be creative: add a free report, add competitions and keep your readers entertained.

3) Maximise your blogs revenue

The great thing is you can make money not just from your book, but also from your blog.

This is called "monetising your blog" where you look to maximise your revenue stream by offering other products on your blog related to your book.

For example if you wrote a book on hypnosis, you could develop an audio CD that buyers could purchase to accompany the book and get practical sessions and guided mediation.

If you wrote a book on yoga you could develop a stunning DVD that buyers of your book could purchase from your blog that takes them through a 1 hour practical session to follow every day. Or if you do not fancy doing that, do a deal with someone who has, who will be delighted to pay you for referring your buyer to their product.

These sorts of products provide a massive boost to your revenue. Imagine if you sold 300 yoga books a month at $2.99, you would get $897. If just 15% of these readers purchased your DVD you would sell an extra 45 DVD at $12.99 yielding an **extra** $584.55 to your profit that month. What if you also sold yoga mats and yoga blocks and some clothing? It goes on and on…

The books are great but BIG money can be made from associated products from your blog. Very exciting stuff and suddenly you can see a real business!

Think about this bigger picture when you are doing your market research and see if you can come up with a niche that lends itself to related product purchases.

4) **Give it enough time to breathe and come to life**

Commit now to NOT throwing the towel in at the first hurdle. There will be tough times ahead and things will seem impossible at the time. Face every challenge with a healthy dose of persistence because usually behind great success lies great challenges. If you listen to any successful author, business person or athlete they all had times when they thought they were not going to make it, where they thought they would quit. But even though the world is full of incredible talent, the winners are always the ones who did not give up.

Remember writing, blogging and publishing is a skill and with practice you will improve and get better, quicker and more efficient. Remember it also takes time for the search engine spiders to find your material. When writing, keep in the back of your mind keywords and phrases your readers and potential buyers might be looking for. It is important that the search engines know you are current, relevant and they aim to make the content as relevant as possible to the search criteria. Scatter relevant keywords throughout your blog to increase the chances of being found by the search engines.

Also remember when your blog is first launched you may have just 5-10 posts published. A year later you may have 300-500 posts published- with links to other bloggers and authors sites and all sorts of interesting interviews, videos and articles. As your blog continues to grow, you will attract more visitors exponentially. In the beginning you will need a bit of a push to gain traction, later, it will be much easier to manage and attract high visitor numbers.

5) **Commit to regular entries**

It is important for new readers to your blog to scan it quickly and know that it is current, that people are leaving comments and that you are regularly posting. A blog whose last post is three months ago is a real turn off. Make sure you post at least 4 times a week but daily if you can.

Content must ALWAYS be unique but you can also ask guest bloggers to post in exchange for a link back to their site.

Check out **http://ezinearticles.com/**. This site has millions of articles on all sorts of topics. Browse it for ideas for your blog. You can submit original, relevant articles there, directing readers back to your site. You can also add articles from here on your blog as long as you include the author box which credits the author.

Make it personal by adding your comments at the end and asking the readers for their input and opinion.

By the way authors do not have to be restricted to nonfiction or fiction books. Many choose to, but imagine if you loved writing fiction and had a few successful books bringing in a decent income. Imagine you also ran for pleasure and to de-stress. You might decide to share this knowledge with the world and have a stab at a nonfiction book on running. You might write a book on how to be a top ultra distance runner. Your book could become a best seller and when you add the sales from DVDs and running gear, you might have doubled your income.

As I said earlier, ideas are everywhere- we just need to capture them.....

Getting serious traffic

So your blog is up and running. You still need to get people to see it, find it and share it with their friends. Add your blog URL to your email signature, tell everyone you know to look at your site, give you their opinion and write a comment if they can. Send readers from your Twitter and Facebook pages to your blog. Keep leaving comments on other related blogs with a link back to your blog.

Seek out opportunities to give a talk at various groups specifically related to your subject area. This is very powerful. A lot of business groups or community groups are always looking for speakers at events. If you give an incredible talk, invite the audience to "like" your Facebook page, comment on your blog, follow you on Twitter and buy your book- you will be amazed how many people do.

You must do some work to get it going but momentum is a wonderful thing- once you start to see activity on your blog, a few sales here and there, it soon gathers momentum and snowballs and often becomes self generating.

So there you have it! Do not get overwhelmed, blogging is a conversation. Liken it to a conversation with your friends- you talk about similar interests, news and gossip and help each other and respond to comments. Do regular, interesting posts, tell the world about your blog and you will see steady and regular growth.

Chapter 4: How To Master the Power of Facebook Marketing

Facebook now has 1.06 billion active monthly users! (March 2013). Although some of us might not like the power and information Facebook has, it would be foolish to ignore this massive market place. It is a magnificent marketing tool and those who use it well see their results sky rocket quicker than anything we have ever seen before.

If you think about it, everything we see, learn, discover and do has to be instantaneous and easy to get. People need instant information and instant solutions to their problems. We need to match this relentless need for information and join in or get left behind.

So this chapter will help you position yourself to create greater brand loyalty and drive higher revenues.

Most business both small and large use Facebook and most people do have a Facebook account and use it to varying degrees.

Here are the 5 steps to take to grab your share of the Facebook market:

Step 1: Set yourself up for major success

If you have not set up an account- stop reading now and go and do this. It is free, easy and quick. When you have done this take some time to search around- see what other people are doing, see what other authors in your niche are doing, how they communicate with their audience. Compare the successful pages with thousands of "likes" with the unsuccessful ones. What is the difference? What sort of information do they convey, how are they engaging with their audience?

Do a search for "20 best brands of Facebook" or "10 top small business pages". Again compare and contrast and take some notes of things you like about a page. How do you become successful? Look at what successful people do and do the same!

Also notice how often they are posting, what content they are posting- video, images or funny jokes? What time of day are they posting? Start today and post 5 items. Start connecting with people and commenting on their posts. Immediately you will notice you get "likes" back as people notice you and wonder what you are up to.

A lot of "best practices" are simply common sense and so to with Facebook. Use it as a conversation, do not preach to your audience or sell to them. Find out what your audience likes, what they want and be genuine.

Step 2: Go viral
Going viral is the aim for every marketer- bar none! It is the holy Grail. This means your fans do your selling for you. It also means you are getting major traffic and exposure for free.

To spread the word and "go viral", you need to post items that people will want to share with their friends and contacts. Once they share your post- it is viewed on their time line and all their friends see it and some of those people who you do not even know will share it- and all their contacts will see it- this is called "going viral". This is your aim and it is the best marketing you can get.

General rules:

1. Post every day if possible. If you are posting only twice a week, it is not enough. Your messages will get lost amongst all the other messages people are looking at every day. The most successful pages post 2-3 times a day. Test your market and see what posts people comment on, what they share and what they like. Notice the time of day you get the best response. Decide what you will do on weekend- a lot of people are on Facebook on weekends so you may not wish to ignore this!
2. Focus on engagement and ask them questions, make it a conversation, go out of your way to find things they might like and share.
3. Have a call to action: Tell them to "like" something or click on the link to your blog or share something. You will be surprised how readily people do this.
4. Balance between over selling and underselling. No one likes being sold to. So do not make every message a sales message or you will turn people off. However if you never mention your blog or your products, you will miss the whole point of building up a loyal fan base. Use the 80/20 rule- 80% content, fun things and interesting points, and 20% mentioning your new book or a special offer on your blog.
5. Make it fun! People are there to find information but mainly to socialise and connect with others and most importantly to have a laugh. If you can make people laugh- you have won them over!

Step 3 Give your page personality

Make your page sound like a real person with lots of charisma.

Take care over the presentation. Be sure to add an intriguing cover page and a decent profile picture of yourself.

Add loads of photos. Pictures paint a thousand words- look for pictures that will liven up your page, entertain your fans, make them laugh and make them want to stay longer. Remember the attention span of someone on the internet now is very short and is reducing every minute. If something doesn't jump off the page and grab them instantly they will move on. Collect reviews and testimonials and add them to your Facebook page.

This all increases your credibility as a serious operator and author they might like to read.

Step 4 Create a content calendar

This is a important step if you think a Facebook strategy will be a core part of your marketing. Take the time to schedule a calendar of material rather than randomly squeeze it into your day. Each weekend plan the content you will post next week. Give each week a theme. Create lots of eye candy, pictures that grab attention and that people will want to share. Be controversial, humorous and engaging.

Schedule promotions throughout the year, link in special offers to seasonal events like Mother's Day, Valentine's Day, Wimbledon final, Thanksgiving and other important dates in your niche.

Step 5 Put on a show

Facebook is all about community. Create your community and events for that community; host a webinar, stream online chat, film a YouTube video, make an effort to create a buzz.

Check out www.facebook.com/ustream for video and showcase your products.

So many millions of people are hungry for your information and Facebook is a major way to reach them free of charge!

Track and Measure
These are the 5 steps to major success on Facebook. As with any business you need to track and measure your success. Analyse what is working and do more of this. Analyse what is not working and do less of that. Facebook very cleverly has provided some tracking tools within it such as number of likes, the reach of a post, how many times each post was seen, number of engaged users and the virality.

Here is a guide as to what is good and bad in Facebook land and what you should be aiming for:

Facebook (English Posts)

Excellent
- Over 3% virality (how viral a post is)
- More than 5000 likes
- More than 700 comments

Good
- 1.5 - 2% virality
- More than 1500 likes
- Over 500 comments

Poor
- Under 1% virality
- Less than 750 likes
- Less than 30 shares

Twitter (English Posts)
- Excellent: More than 100 retweets
- Good: More than 50 retweets
- Poor: Less than 20 retweets

Source: Mozilla Wiki on May 23, 2012

Scan through these statistics on a weekly basis and provide your users more of what they like.

Chapter 5 Critical Internal Marketing (most authors do not know this!)

This chapter reveals the inner workings within Amazon Kindle platform to help you maximise your success. We call it internal marketing as there are several steps you can take within the Kindle platform that almost guarantees your success. Remember that Amazon is *already* spending hundreds of thousands of dollars daily to bring buyers to their platform who are searching for e-books. Your job is to get your book in front of their eyeballs. Then get them to press "buy".

Most of the work has already been done by Amazon- all you have to do is make your book more attractive than the others and optimise its searchability.

Here is how to do it:

E Book Cover

The old saying goes "Never judge a book by its cover" however when most of you will be unknown authors, the cover is the ONLY thing the buyer can judge us on in the first few seconds. It makes sense to spend a bit of time getting this right. The prospect has decided to browse Kindle. They will be scanning loads of books vying for their attention and will decide in a matter of milliseconds whether to look further at your book or move on. Without an eye catching cover, you could lose them before they have even read the title!

I know myself when I scan down through Kindle best sellers or my subject area, I skip over quickly any cover that looks unprofessional or faded or dull. Our eye is drawn to bright colours, clear, clean design that we do not have to decipher. Remember that it will be viewed in thumbnail so it must be clear in small format and some e-readers only support black and white so it must be clear and compelling in these formats also. Think like an app design for an Iphone. The small image MUST catch the eye.

You definitely need to spend time creating the best cover you can. You also need to spend time testing the cover. I test on average 6-10 cover images. This is important. You will not know immediately which cover is best- the buyers will tell you which one is selling. Listen to them.

If your sales are slow, do not assume it is your subject matter, your book or that you are a bad writer. (Yes -you can assume this if you get a lot of returns.) But if you are simply not making the sales it will because your book cover or title are not as good as they need to be. The image attracts the eye balls first then the title closes the deal and makes the sale.

Here is Amazon's fairly helpful information on creating the cover image. If you are NOT a designer, do not try to do this yourself! Outsource it to the professionals listed in the outsource chapter (later) for a small fee. This can cost from $5 to a few thousand dollars. To get the best from outsourced designers you need to give them as much information as possible. You need to manage them. Tell them who your audience will be, which demographic, the themes or message you want your audience to have. Tell them it must look amazing as a postage stamp size and that the title can be seen clearly. Also let them know if you have any special colour requirements or any specific pictures you wish to use.

When you get the cover proof back, be critical, ask for feedback from trusted friends and family. Ask the designer for any changes if you are not completely happy. Most are usually more than happy to make adjustments so their customer is satisfied and will use them again.

Good cover design options are:

- Run a competition on 99designs.com (many designers will come up with a design for you. You browse through hundreds of them and simply choose and pay for the one you like best. Price usually $50-$500)
- Hire someone from www.guru.com or www.odesk.com to design one for you (price usually $20-$50)
- Post your job on www.fiverr.com and get someone to design one for you for $5.

A clever title is worth a million dollars

Let's go back to your potential buyer. Let's assume they like the cover, your book has caught their eye. You have passed the "cover" test and they stay with you long enough to investigate further. The next thing they will pay attention to is the title. Our lives are so busy now and we tend to have short attention spans, most people no longer read at leisure, they scan quickly! Your title must jump off the page and grab them straight away. If they have to think about it, or try to decipher what the message is, they will usually just move onto something easier. Your title must jump out at them, intrigue them, make them laugh or it will lose their attention straight away.

Fiction titles can be a little more obscure and creative as people will usually check out the description quickly before moving on. However for non fiction writers the title must tell them everything they need to know. A short punchy title with a longer more detailed subtitle is best (just like this book!).

For example a book on woodworking could be called "Woodworking: The Complete Illustrated Guide to Working with Wood in just 30 days." The prospect knows they will get a guide that will explain the basics to them, give them some fast results (in just 30 days) with pictures or diagrams to help them through. This title is FAR better than something like "Craftsman and Artisan". This is unclear and does not convey what the book is about. Most people will not spend the time to investigate further they will move on quickly to the next book which catches their eye.

Remember brainstorm for a while, do not make the title the first one you come up with. Write down catchy, sizzling adjectives, active verbs, rhymes, clichés. Try different combinations or words and phrases. Look at the other titles in your genre particularly the best sellers. Obviously do not copy these but it will give you a starting point, then make it better using your own creativity and personality. If you are writing nonfiction, it is best to have a fairly short title then a more descriptive sub title. As always try to use the keyword phrases you identified in chapter 1. The subtitle must also be catchy and aim to sell the benefits to the reader.

Apply considerable thought to this process: maybe 2-3 hours, come up with the best title you can then test it. Test it on people who will be honest – not your sweet lovely friend or your grandma.

Continue to test it after you publish it. Record sales for 2 weeks, then change a word or two in the title, re test it and measure sales. Then change the subtitle and so on. Watch very closely what sells and what grabs the reader's attention. I will say this again- the title is very important. Continue to test, measure and change until you peak at maximum sales. Your readers will quickly let you know what sells.

Formatting and Publishing

Formatting and publishing is a necessary step you must take full responsibility for. In the days when you were signed by a publishing house, they did this. Now you as a self published author must take control of this process. This section reveals the secrets of getting it published on Kindle.

As well as the content of the book itself, you need to think about the other content for the front and back of the book. Pick up any paperback book and look at all the extra work around it besides the content. You need the same material for your e-book.

You may need:

- Table of contents (for nonfiction books)
- Teaser for the front cover
- Book description (the sales page)
- About the author
- Title page
- Copyright page
- Preface
- Afterward
- Appendices ++
- Testimonials and reviews

++ Appendices (or resources section: this can be really useful to help drive traffic to your website and get readers to find your book)

You may decide against some of these sections depending on the nature of your book.

Make sure you write your book in word. Keep it simple using simple fonts like Times New Roman 12pt. If your font and style is messy, it will look unprofessional, it will be difficult to read and it will kill sales.

Use Heading 1 or 2 for your chapter headings; and Heading 2 or 3 for sub chapter headings. Get in the habit of being consistent. Make sure all your new chapters start on a new page – just like in a printed book.

The aim in the back of your mind always should be to have it as simple and clean looking as possible. Clear out any clutter that should not be there. Do not add in headers, footers or special fonts.

Be careful with indent. The Kindle viewing area is not huge- remember the platform your readers will be reading it on, too many indents look messy and will irritate the readers.

Do not bother with page numbers as by the time it is in Kindle format the numbers will not relate to anything significant anyway. The reader can change the font size to suit them. Remember also your audience will be reading your books on all sorts of e-readers- iPad's, Nooks, Kindles and many other brands.

Don't go crazy with fonts or colours. The new e-readers can read colour but remember a lot of people will be reading pure black and white for now.

In terms of formatting, keep your book as generic and simple as possible and you will have better success.

Amazon itself has a pretty comprehensive guide to formatting .

The 3 Best Conversion Tools

You will need to convert your manuscript from a word document to a format that Kindle recognises. There are a number of tools to do this. Here are some of the better ones:

    1)   Calibre

Calibre is a tool that can covert from a huge number of formats to a huge number of formats. Best of all it is free. It is a great e-book library tool as well. Check out their website to get a flavour of all that they do. **http://calibre-ebook.com/**

You can also upload word.doc files directly to the Kindle platform. You can upload html files directly as well. PDF will not upload so do not bother with this one.

    2)   Mobipocket creator

Amazon recommends using mobipocket creator **http://www.mobipocket.com** (mainly because they own it). It is easy and takes less than 5 minutes.

    3)   Kinstant formatter

http://kinstantformatter.com/ is another great tool available but there is a charge for this one. It automatically fixes some formatting issues you may have missed like blank spaces where they shouldn't be. It will also do cool things like creating active chapter headings to the reader can click through straight to their chapter heading of interest without having to scroll through the whole book.

If you want someone else to do the formatting conversion for you, then I use these guys, great value and very efficient. www.kreatorsystems.com

Creating a table of contents designed to sell

The Table of Contents is one of your biggest sales tools for nonfiction books.

Amazon Kindle has an amazing feature which allows the potential reader to "Look Inside" the book and read the first 10%. This means if you have been successful enough to get the prospect this far- they are interested in your book and are just seeking confirmation that you will be providing the answers to the problem they have. When you write your Table of Contents, keep in the back of your mind that this is part of your sales tools. You want to con-firm to the reader that this book will solve their problems, that you are an authority and you will impress them with valuable information they may not have thought of yet. You want to create a feeling in them of "I MUST have this book now!" and have them clicking the "BUY" button without bothering to check the competition.

Also keep in the back of your mind the keyword phrases you identified from the chapter 2. Try to insert a scattering of these in your Table of Contents to ensure your book is found and you are appealing directly to the reader's main problems.

I know myself when looking for nonfiction books I always scan the Table of Contents and place a lot of judgement on it. If the Table of Contents is boring, vague or has spelling errors, I go no further and move onto the next book quickly.

This is how you do it. Simply go to "References" in your word document, then Table of Contents then insert "Table of Contents". The default setting is to show page numbers and hyperlink. Remember you do not want to show page numbers. So untick the "show page numbers" box.

You are done!

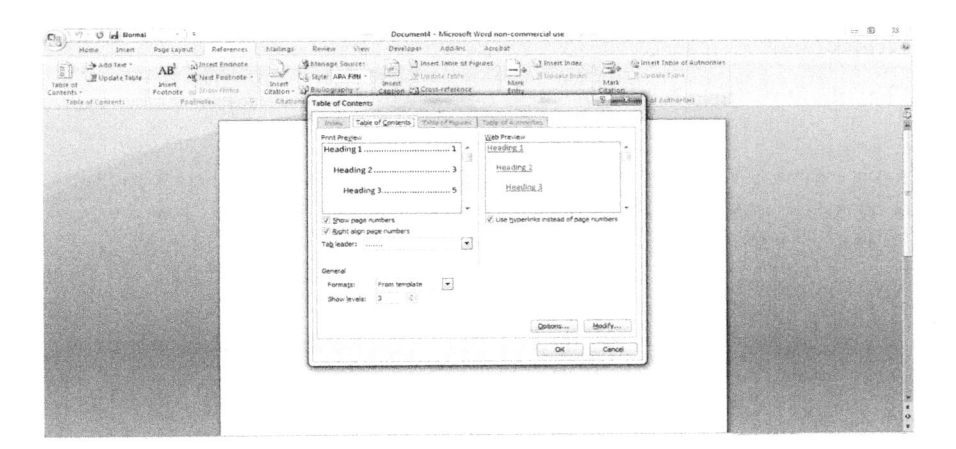

Start each chapter on a new page by hitting insert page break to begin new chapter then do Heading 1 or 2. Keep it consistent whichever one you choose.

Links

You can add links to your text in Kindle. Simply type the text you wish to be linked, highlight the text, right click and select hyperlink from the box.

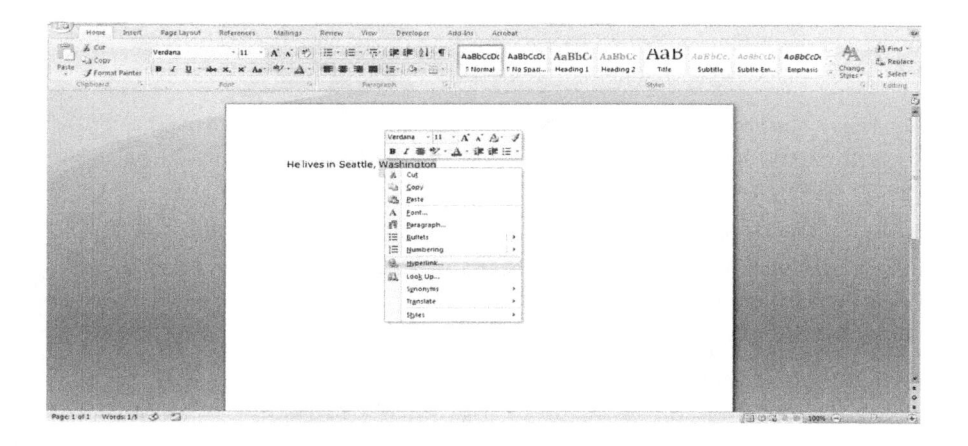

Make sure the existing file or web page is selected and type in the web address you wish to link to. You may wish to link to your blog, to your other books, to another website or to another section of your book.

What about pictures?

Images are fine to use if they add value. Do not use too many, do not use them to pad out the book. Readers see through this straight away. Add images by clicking on "Insert" then "Picture" and browse for the file on your computer.

If you simply copy and paste into your text, the picture will not be seen.

Typical resolution for Kindle images is 300dpi. Again remember simple is best and not that many e readers can see in colour as yet.

You also must have the rights to publish the picture.

Royalties and pricing

Ahh.. royalties...the magic word we all long to hear as authors. Remember pricing is a serious part of your marketing strategy. Your aim is to get maximum **revenue** from your hard work and your fantastic book, not maximum price. The correct price will attract more buyers, the wrong price will turn them off.

Now: there is an important distinction: When you sell direct from your blog, you collect 100% of the revenue and can charge what you like.

When you sell on Amazon you can select 35% or 70% royalty payments. This is fair enough as for their end of the bargain, they are putting your book in front of a massive audience, they upkeep the website, advertise the books for sale (maybe yours one day!), offer related books you might like and they collect and process the money and send you the cash!

To qualify for 70% you must meet Amazon criteria:

1) You must sell your book between $2.99-$9.99
2) It must be original work, ie not public domain

So, I hear you say, that is pretty straight forward- why would anyone choose to receive 35%?

Several reasons: people who want to use their book as lead generation tool. They may wish to distribute the books as quickly as possible to as many people as possible. Amazon's minimum price is £0.99 (though they do offer free promotions). John Locke who made $1 million selling e-books priced his books at 99 cents.

There are also authors who wish to charge premium pricing. They do not wish to diminish the value of their already published hard back book which may sell at $39 or $59 (as is often the case with nonfiction books). Or they might have a book that will sell really well and they feel they can generate more revenue selling less copies but at a higher price.

Clever Pricing Strategy

In the beginning, assuming you are an unknown author, it is best to price your book fairly low. Check out the competition in your niche first and price it just under. The most important thing in the beginning is getting sales under your belt. Once you have momentum you will feel better about the enormous effort you put in writing, proofreading, marketing and publishing your book. You also may start to get some independent reviews which will be very important in getting you noticed and moving up the rankings. The higher ranked you are, the more people see your book and the better your sales will be.

As with selling any product you will need to test different price points and measure, test and measure again.

Remember you are aiming for maximum revenue not greatest price! Test and measure to find the sweet spot.

For example if you do price it at 99 cents, you may sell more but is that enough to generate more revenue than a book selling slightly less numbers but priced at $3.99?

Some authors choose to use a free or 99 cent price strategy initially to get the sales made to launch them into the top 10 best sellers then gradually increase the price by a dollar every two weeks and measure the results. Depending on your genre this can be quite a clever strategy as the most important thing is getting the book seen by people and getting some genuine reviews up straight away.

This is not a failsafe method however and does depend on the type of reader you are looking to attract. Some people will never buy a 99 cent book as the perception is it might be "too cheap" and therefore a low grade book! Other readers buy several 99 cents books because they are cheap but they might never get around to reading them. Sure you have made a sale but if they never read your book, they certainly won't leave you a review or buy your next book!

In the end, this is a judgement call and requires some experimentation. There is not one correct price and you will find even similar books in a similar genre written by you, will have different pricing "sweet spots".

Perceived value of the product

Another way to come to price is to think about what value the product might provide to someone's life and the potential value of the product from the buyer's perspective. There will likely be a significant price difference between a 21 page manual on dating compared with a 500 page dossier on astrophysics. If you sold the dating book for $9.99 you would probably get a lot of returns as 21 pages is not exactly substantial. The book on astrophysics would be amazing value at $9.99 as presumably it would be based on many years of solid research and science. It would probably sell to a small niche market very well at $19.99 or even $39.99!

If you wrote an amazing book on how to be a stock market trader, you would be able to charge a higher fee as the potential rewards of this knowledge might earn the reader tens of thousands of dollars when they apply it.

You will be judged (or crucified) by the reader. If you throw any old thing together and it is a sloppy, unfinished product, you will get refund requests and a reputation of being unprofessional. However if you respect the readers time by producing a quality, professional, compelling piece of work, you will gain huge fan base from honest reviews of the readers and word of mouth referrals.

Remember the reader can return it within 7 days to get a full refund if they did not like it, if they felt ripped off or for any other reason they choose. Luckily most people are honest and are happy to pay $2.99 or $8.99 for a great read or a book that helped them overcome their current problem.

Pricing is an art rather than a science. Continue to test and measure and the true price will reveal itself. Keep a spread sheet and make one change then give it two weeks before you make another change.

Create your author page on Amazon Author Central

This is an opportunity to draw even more readers into your web.

Check out the site: https://authorcentral.amazon.com/

This is where you write a biography on yourself and add your photo – you are now an author!

This is also a sales tool, so take care when writing this section that it grips the reader, they engage with you and they want to buy from you. Do not make the mistake of taking painstaking effort over every word in your novel then blow it all by rushing the author bio.

Paint your personality in vivid language, try to connect with people through author central. Readers who check out this section are looking to determine what sort of person you are to see if they will relate to you and therefore your books.

Remember you have already determined through your initial research who your audience is so make sure you write something that not only appeals to them but simply knocks their socks off!

This is not a place to write a boring resume. Most people will not care than you went to Main Town Elementary School then worked at a fast food chain for 5 years, before working in a supermarket.

Spice it up, be creative and aim to connect. Depending on your genre you might try to make them laugh, be empathetic, or impress them with your knowledge. This section helps give you credibility and overcome any hesitation from the buyer.

Your job here is to make them want to be your friend and want to buy from you. Spend a few hours at least on this job.

In Author central you can also link your bio to your book directly and when your book appears on Amazon it will show your bio on the main sales page.

Enrol in the Amazon KDP select program

This program is a fabulous service by Amazon and makes your book available exclusively to Amazon for a set period. Enrolment is easy and done by the click of one button. You can set a number of promotion days (currently 5) where you make your book available for free to see the effect free downloads have on getting your book seen by as many readers as possible. This is a great strategy for getting your book maximum exposure and moving up the sales rank lists.

Test which days of the week work best for you. I tried my first free promotional period on a week-day. The second time, I tried it on a weekend, where I figured more people would be lazing about on the couch browsing the Kindle Store. The second time around, free downloads were lower overall, but I did see another big increase in downloads after the promotional period ended. This is purely trial and error. The only way you can go wrong is if you do not track your sales and what happens when you try free promotion. There is no strict rule for this- it will depend on your genre, time of day, day of week and a bit of luck!

The KDP program also allows your book to be borrowed for free by KDP premium members. It works like a library service. If your book is borrowed by KDP members, you'll also receive a share of the borrowed royalty pie.

For all the info on the KDP Select Program have a browse around here. It is explained very well by Amazon. **https://kdp.amazon.com/self-publishing/**

Look Inside Feature

Amazon gives the reader a chance to sample the first 10% of the book. This is a fantastic opportunity to showcase your wares! Do not waste this opportunity by making them wade through lots of random, irrelevant stuff like copyright pages, acknowledgements and so on. Do you really need 6-8 pages of "fluff" before you get to the sizzle?

The more clicks someone has to go through to get to your product, the more chance you have of losing them.

I discovered this myself when I did not pay much attention to this feature. I had lots of acknowledgements and forwards at the beginning, a factual Table of Contents and an average introduction. I had left the "sizzle" too late in the book and thought the book description would do most of the selling. But no - this feature is too powerful to be ignored.

Once I realised the power of the "Look Inside" feature, I stripped out everything but the bare essentials in the front so the reader got straight to the Table of Contents and I made sure the first 10% of the book enticed the reader and confirmed to them that this book would give them what they wanted. My sales increased by over 516%!

Focus on connecting with the reader straight away and use strong keywords to demonstrate you know what you are talking about and can give them the answers to their problems. Even though the first 10% is the first part of your book and must flow smoothly with the rest, it is still a sales tool at this stage. Remember, the reader has not yet purchased and they are assessing whether your book will be worthwhile.

If you are writing a fiction book, set the scene straight away and write enough to leave them salivating for more pages. The prospect will be thinking "Does it move me?" "Do I like these characters?" The first 10% of the book should leave them desperate for more and having them hitting the buy button immediately to find out what happens!

In a nonfiction book, the prospect should pretty much come straight to the Table of Contents which should already be impressing them, enticing them, confirming that this book will give them solutions and have them hovering over the buy button! I know myself I have often bought books straight from the Table of Contents as I can see clearly they will be covering the exact information I need and I am so excited that I want the book right now.

Spend time making your Table of Contents interesting and informative and your first few chapters or introduction appealing.

For example: A book on "How To Swim Better" might have chapters like:

- The pull through
- The entry
- Benefits of two sided breathing

How much better would the book seem if the chapters heading were titled:

- Master your pull through in just 30 seconds
- 3 gym exercises that will guarantee 15% improved swim times in the next 21 days
- Two sided breathing from the former Olympic champion

Remember the first 10 % is the "sales" document. Obviously it needs to be readable and make sense. Your goal of the first line is to make them want to read the second line. The goal of the second line is to make them want to read the third line and so on. Leave out fluff, pack it with high value content that demonstrates you are the expert and leave them wanting more.

Get amazing reviews- every time!

One of your key jobs as being in charge of marketing and publishing for your new empire is doing EVERYTHING you can to get reader reviews. Good reader reviews sell more books!

People are more likely to leave a review for you when they are in the "warm zone" just after finishing the book. Imagine they have just finished your gripping last chapter and are glowing in amazement thinking "What a great author, I loved that book, maybe I will have a look for anything else he/she has written tomorrow!" Well folks, as we all know, tomorrow rarely comes. We wake up tomorrow and start another day of work, training, emails, phone calls, we can hardly remember yesterday or what we read unless something prompts us to do so. Reviews are hard to come by as most people are "too busy" and do not bother.

The statistics are terrible: approximate figures of those who leave reviews are 0.0001%.

So we MUST encourage the reader to leave a review straight away. And we must make it easy for them to do so.

Good reviews have an amazing power to help sales. But friendly warning: **1 star reviews depress sales more than 5 star reviews lift it.**

It is a good idea to ask your family and friends to leave genuine reviews to get the ball rolling. Make sure you tell them honest feedback is required, not supercilious gush! If you see a product with 5 star gushy, over the top rubbish, you would suspect foul play and definitely NOT buy the product. Aim for a good mix of 4 and 5 stars with a couple of 3 stars. Make sure your family and friends have actually bought the book! If there are 2-3 reviews already there, it makes it more likely that the average reader will leave a review.

One of the most powerful pieces of real estate is the end of the book. Amazon has a "Before You Go" feature which prompts the reader to immediately rate your book and make a comment. It also links to Facebook and Twitter which is fantastic for enhancing your social media profile and helping your book to go viral.

Make sure there is not a lot of "junk" at the back of your book like index, appendices (unless absolutely critical) or afterward. You want to invite them immediately to leave a review and ask them directly to do so.

Something like "I really hope you enjoyed reading this book. I certainly enjoyed writing it. It would really help me if you would spare a minute or two to leave a review".

Then leave a link for them to click on.

Your number of reviews will sky rocket and so will your sales as the more reviews you have, the more people are likely to buy because of social proof. You are removing an obstacle to buying which is "I have never heard of this author. How do I know if it will be any good?" If 159 people have given you positive reviews, you will sell more books than a book with 2 reviews- every time!

A word of warning: the only way this can back fire is if your book is NOT very good. You will certainly get a lot of reviews but if they are bad reviews- your book will never see the light of day! So take the time to write the BEST quality book you can! Also if you do get multiple bad reviews which are all saying the same thing- make the effort to critically examine you book, see if their criticism if valid and improve your book.

If you are a multiple book author, this is the time where you invite them to purchase more of your books. You add a section called "More books by James Calthorpe".....with a link to your Amazon purchase page.

You could also invite them to sign up to your monthly newsletter.

Eg Questions or comments for James? Please email me at james@ebookmoneymaker.com

You want them on your list so you control the dialogue, your promotions, you can upgrade them to your other services, like consulting or seminars. Or simply get ready to email them when you have your next book ready to go.

Chapter 6 Are other traditional forms of marketing any good?

So now you have Twitter, Facebook page and your blog set up which is spreading the word via external marketing. You have also completed your internal marketing to make sure anyone searching on Amazon itself can find you easily, what else can you do?

Do not forget traditional forms of marketing that are still very important in getting as many eye balls to view your books and buy as possible.

Forums

There are many forums out there for every genre and interest group possible. Search for them on your favourite search engine typing in "your niche topic + forums" to the search bar. Engaging with others in your field is a really good way of getting the word out about your book and establishing yourself as an expert.

Always seek to be helpful, genuine and interested. Join a forum with the intention of helping others. Do not go on there and spam the forum or you will be kicked out and other members will remember your name and definitely not buy from you.

Seek to give first then rewards will come back to you hundred fold.

Create your signature that will appear every time you post. Doing this will create links back to your post. Also post a couple of questions to stimulate discussion and look for other questions posed and answer those as best you can. If you come across as a genuine person, people will look up your site and probably buy your book.

Forums are especially useful for non-fiction writers as the subject can be specific to your book.

Press releases

Writing and sending out press releases can seem like hard work but it pays huge dividends. It can also get you on some very highly ranked and high traffic websites and therefore create a lot of exposure. Press releases done well create visibility, a buzz and conveys credibility. This means it will generate sales!

Be on the lookout for breaking news, or stories of interest and write an article on it related to your site, your book and give your opinion.

Add controversy if possible as the media love this and you will get more column inches.

Try these ones as a start but there are many more...

www.prweb.com

www.prfree.com

www.prnewswire.com

These sites are leaders in online news and press releases. They are used by close to 100,000 organisations of all sizes to increase traffic to their websites, to improve their visibility in the public eye and to improve their search engine rankings.

Blog links

An awesome way to get more traffic is to have other highly trafficked sites referencing your site and pointing their readers to you. To make this happen you need great content. This is where great video or podcasts come into their own. If you think about it, the greatest way we consume information now is through video or audio. Of course we still read a lot but if you can make your information come alive- people will flock to you.

Just as you are continually searching for high quality, awesome content to add to your blogs, other blog owners are also searching for great content to add to theirs. If you have something which their readers will find interesting they will be more than happy to post it on their site.

Search out high traffic blogs and make sure you subscribe so you get notified as soon as they post a new article. Be the first to comment straight away - making sure your blog link appears in your signature box. You will get people immediately checking you out and going to your site. Make sure the comments are relevant, useful and genuine. Gone are the days where you could simply say "great post!" or "thanks for that!" Actually read their post and write an intriguing paragraph or two about it.

More Social Media- do I need to do ALL of it?

The list of social media sites is truly endless and there are more and more social media sites being born every day. For example YouTube, Digg, Squidoo, Technorati, Delicious and so on. If your book lends itself to YouTube video then create one (this is the second biggest search engine on the web), but there will be a significant cost to getting a professional video filmed so if you do not have a budget then create something simple and interesting. Sometimes the home made ones do more damage than not doing one at all so be careful!

You need to make the decision if it is worth it. My advice is if you have a functioning blog, several books already published and a profitable "back end" of several products lined up to sell on your blog, the investment in a YouTube video is worth it.

If you are just starting out with only one book at $0.99, do not invest big bucks in this step yet. Focus on the basics and get them right first!

Of course everyone's time is limited so I advise you to have a quick scan through the other social sites and see if any appeal. Definitely get moving with Twitter, Facebook and your blog and any others are a bonus. It is a good idea to scan them quickly once a week and see what the trending topics are as they are often a good source of content for your blog posts.

Chapter 7 Neglected parts to most businesses

Outsourcing

Outsourcing is a necessary step some writers take to grow their business faster. It allows you to focus on what you do best and outsource the rest. For most writers, the part they love and are brilliant at is the writing- and no one else should or could do that for you. This is unique! If someone else did this for you, you would lose the magic that your readers love. However you might outsource the building of websites, blogs, the graphic design, sometimes even the leaving comments on other blog sites.

A word of warning though: In the beginning do everything yourself! I mean it. Even though it takes a while to do it all, go through the steps, it is really important that you understand what is involved at each step before you get others to do it.

For some of you, one or two books in the area you are passionate about will be enough. There is enough to do to continue to update your blogs, Facebook pages, Twitter and generate a nice income from this. Writing books will establish you as the expert in your field and if you do the marketing right by following the steps in this book (assuming your book is great) you will get fabulous sales and be able to get more lucrative work by calling yourself a "bestselling author".

I have seen some friends of mine double their speaking fee overnight as they put what they knew on paper, wrote a book and did their marketing right. They are now recognised as being a "bestselling author" and command much higher fees.

So even one or two books are worth doing and will change your life if done properly.

However if you wish to turn yourself into a multimillion dollar publishing empire and have multiple books in multiple areas, you will need to get help. If you do not- YOU will be the stumbling block in your business. You will be the one holding up proceedings.

However once you are familiar and have a good grip on everything, you will be able to build your empire a whole lot quicker if you outsource some of the tasks.

Common areas to outsource are the marketing, the writing of articles for your website or blog, the linking of blogs, the website management and responding to comments.

Here are some sites to check out where you can get very reasonable, highly skilled workers:

https://www.elance.com/

https://www.odesk.com/

http://www.guru.com/

http://fiverr.com/

http://99designs.co.uk/

It is up to you to do your own due diligence when taking on remote workers but I have used some for website design, blog building and graphic design and never had a problem.

You can build this business up to a six figure a year income very quickly- I am not joking here! Some people are earning **six figures a month** from e-books and publishing. If you are serious about this, you cannot be at your desk taking 8 months to write each book and 4 months to get all the marketing sorted. Think of yourself as managing a publishing empire.

You will always be the one creating the ideas, researching the market, the trends, seeing what's hot and what is likely to sell. This is your role as CEO of this fledging empire. Do not outsource this role. Without this, you do not have a business.

Using these sites I have provided for you- you can meet and hire skilled people from all over the world who may not charge as much as people in your own country. It is a global marketplace- use the power of the internet to your advantage.

It is best to give out a small job first, check the quality of the work and then gradually increase the size of the workload.

Remember that every empire starts small. Do not get carried away if you are just starting out. Focus on getting the first book done and marketed correctly. Follow through all the steps. Get some sales, encourage reviews and track your stats each month. You should see growth in your sales every month. For some books it will stabilise into average monthly sales. The first book will be the hardest and take the longest as every step is new and you do not have confidence yet. Get the first book done and operating successfully, then the second before you think of outsourcing. After this, start to dip your toe in the water and look to build a dynamic team you can trust and rely on.

Keep Expenses low

For some of you, writing books is a passion and you are not doing it for money or fame or recognition, but then again if that was the case you would probably not be reading this book!

For most of you, you are trying to gain extra income, extra sales and improve your financial life in some way whether supplemental or replacement of your full time income.

This is a business. You will need to see some profit at the end of the day. Once you deduct your expenses- proof reading, marketing, design, distribution, your time, what is actually left?

Sales are hard to predict at the beginning so it is very important initially to keep your expenses low. Remember never to invest money you don't have, never borrow to publish a book. You might never earn a penny! Of course following the methods in this book you will be fine and way ahead of everyone else but be prudent until the sales come in. Then re-invest your **profits** to improve your design, improve your blog or outsource any tasks you do not wish to do.

For example do not spend thousands of dollars getting the best cover designed by an award winning designer. For now try to get the best one you can for around $50 or less. **Once you have some profit** you can then invest this back into upgrading the cover. Do not spend money you do not have!

Segment Your Day

As with any business, you are in charge of a lot of tasks. It is easy to become overwhelmed. You are in charge of writing winning books, researching the next blockbuster, keeping up with fresh blog updates, Facebook posts, growing your Twitter account, responding to your emails, finance and operations.

Segment your day so you are structured. For example you may do four hours of writing per day, one hour of Twitter, one hour of blogging and one hour Facebook. Once a week you reviews sales for the week and plan the week ahead. Whatever works for you, but once you set the plan- stick to it. Do not suddenly get distracted by Facebook and accidentally spend two hours checking out the latest video game or YouTube advert. Remember this is work time, be efficient and stick to the plan. Once a month review the plan and if it needs to change, do it then.

On every email you send out, make sure your company name is there plus a link to your blog and an Amazon link to every book you have written. This is further free marketing and brand awareness. Again it is free and very effective. You will be surprised how many people check out your books when they receive a direct email from you.

CHAPTER 8: Here we go…!

You now have the tools, fellow authors. You can succeed.

It's not difficult to publish your book onto the Kindle Store.

It is not difficult to publish your book on your own blog.

It is not difficult to post one or two items a day on Twitter and Facebook or write four blog posts a week.

It is not difficult to search out related blogs and comment on them leaving a valuable link back to your website.

None of this is difficult by itself!

It was more difficult studying for your final school exams or writing your best man speech or completing the 100 mile ultra-marathon.

These things are difficult!

Writing and publishing is not difficult.

Hard work yes, but not difficult.

Discipline required yes, but not difficult.

What can go wrong?

There are three simple steps to take to ensure great success.

1. Find out what people want (market research)//
2. Give them what they want (write the book)
3. Tell them where to get it (marketing)

That's it!

It really is that simple. It goes wrong when people do not follow the steps.

For example even after reading this book, at least half of you will NOT do the market research. You will be so excited to get on with your "great idea" and write the book, spend four or five months toiling over your manuscript only to find after all that, nobody buys it.

Do the market research, you will almost guarantee enormous success if you know before you start that you have 50,000 people a day already searching for information contained in your book.

Do not over complicate this. Do your research then write the best darn book you can, full of passion, flow and energy. Your aim is to wow your reader and impress them. Take care over your sentences, your words and your grammar. Plan your book so it flows in a logical way. Some authors get stuck at the writing part and call it "writers block". If this happens to you a good trick is not to stare at a white screen but to step away, sit in a quiet place or go for a walk. Take your phone with a recording device or a notebook, and when you are relaxed just let your ideas flow. Simply talk into the recorder or scribble down ideas that pop into your head.

When you get back to your desk, start writing. You can polish it later, for now just start writing and remove all distractions, close the door, turn your phone and email off and do not get up until you complete the goal you set in your plan e.g. 2000 words or three chapters a day.

Once written, edited, and proof read your job is to tell the world about it and where to find it.

Most authors are not great at publicity and fall down at this step. They think readers will magically find their beloved book. No my friends, you must put it out there in front of their face.

However these days, it simply could not be easier. You do not have to fly around the country on a massive high budget radio tour or make speeches and do loads of book signings. You just have to do daily and consistent social media, online PR, connect with people and build online relationships. And it is FREE! This is a major opportunity given to our generation via technology that previous generations did not have access to. Do not squander it- soak it up and milk it for all it is worth.

If your book is good enough and intriguing enough, readers will buy and may become loyal fans lining up to buy your next book before it is even written!

For most of us this process will not result in instant riches- very few things do.

But if you follow the steps in the book, you will be able to see a consistent, rising second income that may very quickly overtake your primary income.

It is possible your first book will generate enough income to pay the monthly car payments, maybe the second book earns enough to pay the house payments, the third book might just cover your food bills.

Imagine that- in just three books, you may be financially free. Your basic living expenses could be all paid for month in, month out. Of course your goal may be much bigger and you may want to turn this into a major empire. You now have all the tools and strategies to do so.

Just keep going- one day you may be noticed by a journalist who does a piece on you and suddenly you have 10,000 sales in one day! Trust me, it happens.

Once launched, you will start a process of testing and measuring until you find the sweet spot. Remember to only change one thing at a time or you will have no idea of what worked. Test different covers, different titles, different price points, different author profiles and different book descriptions. Allow two weeks to allow the changes to take effect, record your sales figures every single day at the same time. You will be building up some important data and get a good feel of the book. But do take the time test, measure and change a few things until a few months later you are generating maximum revenue.

If you sell a lot but get many returns, you must face facts that your book is simply not good enough. Do a serious re edit- look at content, flow, font, grammar, pay a professional proof reader to tear it apart and re submit it.

Do not be too proud to do this. With some minor tweaking, your next version may hit the jackpot.

What if it all goes right?

Do not let the magnitude of the task at hand overwhelm you. Remember focus on one step at a time and do not stop until this step is done.

The first book will be the hardest because it is all new.

Once you have gone through the process once or twice, you will be flying and desperate to get three, four, then five books out the door.

For some of you the first book many knock conservative figures out of the park! You may have hit a genre that is the next big thing and be raking in £25,000 a month.

Focus on sales, one at a time, focus on getting reviews, tell as many friends about your book as possible. Stay positive, when you get this right, your life will change!

You have a real chance here to make a substantial income.

Grab it with both hands!

Best wishes for your every success- and do email me your success stories, I love hearing from you,

James

james@ebookmoneymaker.com

I hope you enjoyed this book, got some great ideas and found it really helpful. If so, please spare one minute and leave me a review. I would really appreciate it and wish you well with your writing career.